END TIMES

ARE YOU PREPARED?

STUART PATTICO

MINISTRY IN ART PUBLISHING
communicating excellence

COPYRIGHT © 2009 STUART PATTICO

The right of Stuart Pattico to be identified as author of this work has been asserted by him in accordance with the Copyright, Designs, and Patents Act 1988.

All rights reserved. No part of this publication may be produced, distributed, or transmitted in any form or by any means, including photocopying, recording, or other electronic or mechanical methods, without the prior written permission of the publisher, except in the case of brief quotations embodied in critical reviews and certain other noncommercial uses permitted by copyright law. For permission requests, contact the publisher, addressed "Attention: Permissions Coordinator" at the email address below:

Ministry In Art Publishing Ltd
email: publishing@ministryinart.com
website: miapublishing.com

Unless otherwise indicated, Biblical quotations are from the Holy Bible, New King James Version © 1982 Thomas Nelson, Inc.

Quotations marked NIV are taken from the HOLY BIBLE, NEW INTERNATIONAL VERSION. Copyright © 1973, 1978, 1984 by International Bible Society. Used by permission of Hodder and Stoughton Ltd, a member of the Hodder Headline Plc Group. All rights reserved. "NIV" is a registered trademark of International Bible Society. UK trademark number 1448790.

Quotations marked KJV are from the Holy Bible, King James Version.

ISBN: 978-0-9560996-9-3

Cover Design: Allan Sealy
www.miadesign.com

ACKNOWLEDGEMENTS

To my beautiful wife, Andrea: thank you so much for your continued love and support, and for proofreading this manuscript. I love you.

Special thanks also to my good friend, Robert Houslin, whose feedback upon reviewing this manuscript was much appreciated.

Most of all, praise, glory and honour be to my God and Father. You are the Rock in my life and I love You forever.

CONTENTS

FOREWORD
INTRODUCTION
CHAPTER 1 – SIGNS OF THE TIMES
CHAPTER 2 – GLOBALISATION
CHAPTER 3 – EUROPE
CHAPTER 4 – ECUMENISM
CHAPTER 5 – THE MARK OF THE BEAST
CHAPTER 6 – YOUR FINANCIAL SECURITY IN THE LAST DAYS
CHAPTER 7 – ISRAEL
CHAPTER 8 – A NEW HEAVEN AND A NEW EARTH
CHAPTER 9 – WILL YOU BE READY?
CONTACT INFORMATION AND ENDNOTES

FOREWORD

Stuart Pattico is an itinerant minister who bears the weight of the anointing to teach, preach and write. Stuart writes with perspective, objectivity and clarity.

His thriving ministry is the result of a heart that is captive to the words of God and a will that is obedient to the mind of God. Stuart's intention in this book is to inform, encourage, engage and strengthen the faith of his readers.

In what is an insightful and timely book, Stuart brings together relevant, important and up-to-date information, in relation to world events and what the Bible has to say about 'end times' prophecy. Without doubt, we are living in the 'last days', a fact demonstrative of the cataclysmic nature of our times and a drive towards 'globalisation'.

At a time like this, when the elderly, middle aged and even the young who have less experience to go on, are sensing and saying that there are changes taking place in the world which have never been seen before; I urge all believers to read this book, prayerfully, and carefully for in it you will find food for the soul and Biblical answers to the questions of our time.

Bishop Lenford Rowe
Church of God of Prophecy, South London Regional Overseer

INTRODUCTION

Events in society, politics, religion, technology and the environment, all indicate that the scene is being set for the fulfilment of Biblical prophecy.

My interest in end time events began when a prophecy teacher conducted several sessions at what was then my local church. I was stirred by the things I heard, and began to research the matter for myself.

Some time after that, I entered the ministry, and eventually doors began to open for me to teach on end time prophecy. Some of what I have shared is contained in this book.

This short book is not an in-depth study or an overview of end time prophecy. Instead, it is a small collection of observations. These observations have brought me to a simple conclusion: the things that God said would happen in the last days are already happening.

To be forewarned is to be forearmed. It is my prayer that the information in this book will help to prepare you for the days ahead, and encourage you to be ready for the coming of our Lord Jesus Christ.

END TIMES
ARE YOU PREPARED?

SIGNS OF THE TIMES

008

In Matthew 24, Mark 13, and Luke 21, Jesus gave us several things to look out for, which would indicate that we were approaching the end of the age. It is remarkable that as we look at the world today, many of these things are happening before our very eyes! In this first chapter, we will review some of these 'signs of the times' from Jesus, as well as one mentioned by Paul. The accuracy of Jesus' predictions should not surprise us. Eighty percent of all the Bible's predictions have already happened[1], and the remaining twenty will certainly be fulfilled at the appropriate time.

THE GOSPEL PREACHED IN EVERY NATION

Jesus predicted that,

> "this gospel of the kingdom will be preached in all the world as a witness to all the nations, and then the end will come."
> (Matthew 24:14)

Christianity started small – with Jesus and then His disciples, but it is now a global faith that continues to grow. Christianity is now the majority religion in many countries.

GREAT INTERNATIONAL WARS

Jesus also predicted that there would be many wars:

"You will hear of wars and rumours of wars, but see to it that you are not alarmed. Such things must happen, but the end is still to come. Nation will rise against nation, and kingdom against kingdom."
(Matthew 24:6-7, NIV)

This has certainly come true. Here are just some of the wars of last (20th) century:

FRENCH INDOCHINA (1946 –1954)
MEXICAN REVOLUTION (1910)
SPANISH CIVIL WAR (1936 –1939)
FRENCH-ALGERIAN WAR (1954 –1962)
AFGHANISTAN (1979 – 1989)
RUSSO-JAPANESE WAR (1904 –1905)
RIFFIAN WAR (1921 – 1926)
FIRST SUDANESE CIVIL WAR (1955 – 1972)
RUSSO-POLISH WAR (1919 – 1921)
NIGERIAN-BIAFRAN WAR (1967 –1970)
SECOND WORLD WAR (1939 – 1945)
FIRST WORLD WAR (1914-1918)
KOREAN WAR (1950 – 1953)
CHINESE CIVIL WAR (1927 – 1950)
VIETNAM WAR (1959 - 1975)
IRAN-IRAQ WAR (1980-1988)

RUSSIAN CIVIL WAR (1917 - 1923)
CHACO WAR (1932 - 1935)
SECOND ITALO-ABYSSINIAN WAR (1935-1936)
GULF WAR (1990 - 1991)

When I last checked, at that time there were 38 armed conflicts in 28 countries.

FAMINE AND DISEASE

Jesus predicted that,

"... there will be famines, pestilences..."
(Matthew 24:7)

Today, one in nearly seven people do not get enough food to be healthy and lead an active life. This makes hunger and malnutrition the number one risk to health worldwide.[2]

Approximately 2 million people died from AIDS in 2007. More than 25 million people have died from AIDS since 1981.[3]

Today, 1.3 billion people live in extreme poverty. Tonight, 800 million will go to bed hungry. This year, 12 million children will die before their fifth birthday. In the developing world, one child dies every three seconds because of the basic lack of safe water, healthcare, shelter or food.[4]

Scientists have recorded 1,043 tsunamis in the 20th century. The Indian Ocean tsunami of 2004 caused more devastation than all the previous 20th century tsunamis combined.

EARTHQUAKES

Jesus said:

> *"There will be... earthquakes in various places. All these are the beginning of sorrows."*
> (Matthew 24:7-8)

Since 1990, the number of earthquakes has steadily increased. There were almost twice as many earthquakes in 2004 than in 1990. In the 1980's there were 1085 earthquakes between magnitude 6 and 9.9. In the 1990's there were 1492. Between 2000 and 2009, there have already been 1480, and at the time of writing, we are not yet half way through 2009.[5]

TSUNAMIS

Jesus predicted that,

"...nations will be in anguish and perplexity at the roaring and tossing of the sea."
(Luke 21:25, NIV)

Scientists have recorded 1,043 tsunamis in the 20th century.[6] The Indian Ocean tsunami of 2004 caused more devastation than all the previous 20th century tsunamis combined.

DECLINE IN MORAL AND ETHICAL STANDARDS, COMBINED WITH OUTWARD RELIGION

Paul warned Timothy by writing:

> "But know this, that in the last days perilous times will come: For men will be lovers of themselves, lovers of money, boasters, proud, blasphemers, disobedient to parents, unthankful, unholy, unloving, unforgiving, slanderers, without self-control, brutal, despisers of good, traitors, headstrong, haughty, lovers of pleasure rather than lovers of God, having a form of godliness but denying its power. And from such people turn away!"
> (2 Timothy 3:1-5)

Anyone who has watched the news, or read a newspaper can see that the above quotation from the Bible is an accurate description of society today. Indeed, cities are filled with crime, children are disobedient to parents, and our world is filled with brutality. Many people are even afraid to walk the streets or let their children out to play. It has been said that greed has been a major cause of the current economic crisis. A lack of self-control is evident from the high number of teenage pregnancies. According to the Office for National Statistics, between 1998 and 2007, there were at least 395,264 under-18 pregnancies in England, almost half of which led to abortion. In the same period, there were 74,942 under-16 pregnancies in England, more than half of which led to an abortion.[7]

HATRED TOWARDS CHRISTIANS

Jesus warned His followers that:

> "... they will deliver you up to tribulation and kill you, and you will be hated by all nations for My name's sake."
> (Matthew 24:9)

It is estimated that in the 20th century, more Christians died for their faith than in the previous 19 centuries combined.

It has been said that an estimated 160,000 believers were martyred in 1996, and countless others were subjected to unimaginable horrors. Furthermore, it has been observed that the persecution appears to be escalating exponentially.

One Christian dies for their faith every 3 minutes.[8] Over 200 million Christians in at least 60 countries are denied fundamental human rights solely because of their faith.[9] This may be quite a surprise to those who live in the West, but persecution is particularly strong in China, Sudan, and many Muslim countries.

In addition to the above 'signs of the times', there are many other contemporary trends, which indicate that we are in the last days. These include trends in technology, events in Europe, the Middle East, and the rest of the world. In the next chapter, we will start with globalisation, and briefly explore how it relates to end time prophecy.

END TIMES
ARE YOU PREPARED?

GLOBALISATION

GLOBALISATION

The Bible reveals that in the last days, there will arise a world leader, who is commonly known as the antichrist. This leader will be an evil man: he will blaspheme God, persecute and kill God's people, exalt himself above God, sit in the temple as though he were God, and will be worshipped by many. The book of Revelation also reveals that this ruler will have global power:

> *It was granted to him [the antichrist] to make war with the saints and to overcome them. And authority was given him over every tribe, tongue, and nation.*
> *(Revelation 13:7)*

The world is already being prepared for such a man to arise, and have authority over the whole world. Today, there is frequent mention of 'globalisation'. This word refers to the people of the world being unified into a single society so that they can function together. A similar thought is encapsulated in the phrase, 'new world order', which envisions the uniting of the world's superpowers in order to secure and maintain global peace and economic stability. It would seem that such a new world order can only come about through a one-world government. Should the one-world government co-operate with its leader, such a leader would have great global power.

Amongst world leadership today, there is a definite drive towards globalisation and the establishment of a new world order. For example, the Council of Foreign Relations (CFR) is an independent foreign policy group. Richard Haass, the current president of the CFR, wrote an article in 2006 called "State sovereignty must be altered in globalized era". In it, he stated:

> "...states must be prepared to cede some sovereignty to world bodies if the international system is to function... Globalization thus implies that sovereignty is not only becoming weaker in reality, but that it needs to become weaker. States would be wise to weaken sovereignty in order to protect themselves..."[10]

The thought of ceding sovereignty to world bodies is becoming increasingly acceptable. The Bible reveals that "ten kings" will yield their power to the antichrist:

> The ten horns which you saw are ten kings who have received no kingdom as yet, but they receive authority for one hour as kings with the beast. These are of one mind, and they will give their power and authority to the beast. (Revelation 17:12-13)

In recent history, via the example of the European Union (EU), we have seen nations slowly yield some of their sovereignty to a higher power. National culture and identity is thus being weakened. However, this is not merely an EU trend, it is a global trend. Today, national culture is being sublimated to a series of 'world' themed events, which weaken people's national pride and make them 'world citizens'. We commonly hear of 'One World Week', 'World Book Day', 'Global Village' etc. Also, organisations such as the International Organisation for Standardization (ISO) and the International Monetary Fund (IMF) are helping the world move in this direction. The ISO sets various international standards, and the IMF works to foster global monetary cooperation. Indeed, the DfEE (Department for Education and Employment) document on *Developing a global dimension in the school curriculum* (DfEE 2000) describes its purpose as:

> "...to show how a global dimension can be incorporated into both the curriculum and the wider life of the school. This means that the content of what is taught is informed by international and global matters, so preparing pupils to live their lives in a global society." [11]

On November 10th 2008, the Telegraph reported that the British Prime Minister, Gordon Brown, "is to call on fellow world leaders to create a 'truly global society' following the current worldwide economic crisis".[12] At the time of writing, the world is experiencing a global economic crisis. However, this crisis will only further the cause of globalisation so that the prophecies of God's Word may be fulfilled. As Gordon Brown later said in January 2009:

> "...we could view the threats and challenges we face today as the difficult birth-pangs of a new global order - and our task now as nothing less than making the transition through a new internationalism to the benefits of an expanding global society... making the necessary adjustment to a better future and setting the new rules for this new global order." [13]

In a similar pattern to the EU, the nations of this world will yield their sovereignty to a new world government. One day, the leader of the one-world government will be the antichrist. But how will the one-world government work? Some have suggested that the world will be split into ten regions, and that the ten kings mentioned in Revelation 17:12-13, will be the rulers of these ten regions. According to this theory, these ten rulers will yield their power to the antichrist. The Club of Rome is a global think tank that brings together influential and prominent people to contribute to world improvement. Interestingly, a 1974 report to the Club of Rome called *Mankind at the Turning Point* divided the world into ten interdependent regions.[14] These ten regions were as follows:

NORTH AMERICA
WESTERN EUROPE
JAPAN
OTHER CAPITALIST ECONOMIES (AUSTRALIA, NEW ZEALAND, SOUTH AFRICA, ISRAEL)
EASTERN EUROPE & U.S.S.R.
CHINA
NORTH AFRICA AND THE MIDDLE EAST
LATIN AMERICA
TROPICAL AFRICA
SOUTH & SOUTHEAST ASIA

Will the ten kings who give their power to the antichrist be rulers of these ten regions? Time will tell, and I certainly will not be dogmatic about that. Whether or not that will be the case, it is clear that the world is heading towards a new world order. As Gordon Brown said after the conclusion of the London 2009 G20 Summit:

> "I think a new world order is emerging with the foundation of a new progressive era of international co-operation" [15]

A new world order is coming. Many of the world leaders who are working towards this end may have good intentions e.g. world peace, economic stability etc. Unfortunately, as the saying goes, 'the road to hell is paved with good intentions'. One day, the global leader of the new world order will be the antichrist. In the next chapter we will look at the role Europe has to play in this.

EUROPE

In the last chapter, we very briefly looked at globalisation and the formation of a new world order. There are many who believe that the European Union (EU) is the first stage in forming the new world order and the one-world government. A Congress of Europe, meeting at the Hague in 1948, declared that **the creation of a United Europe was an essential element in the creation of a united world.** [16]

Former EU President, Romano Prodi, published a paper called "Strategic Objectives 2000-2005; Shaping the New Europe." In it he says:

> *"What we are aiming at, therefore, is a new kind of global governance to manage the global economy and environment.*
>
> *Europe's model of integration... is a quarry from which ideas for global governance can and should be drawn. We must promote this, while devising just and sustainable strategies at world level."* [17]

Thus it would indeed appear that the formation of the EU is bringing the world one step closer to the new world order, over which the antichrist will one day rule.

The EU is a political and economic union consisting

of 27 countries. Its founding document is called the Treaty of Rome, and was signed in 1957 by six countries.

It is interesting that the founding document is called the Treaty of Rome. 'Rome' also symbolically appears on the EU flag. You will notice that the EU flag consists of a blue background with a circle of twelve yellow stars. The twelve stars do not represent countries, as there are presently 27 countries in the EU. What then do the stars represent? According to the official EU website,

> "In various traditions, twelve is a symbolic number representing perfection. It is also, of course, the number of months in a year and the number of hours shown on a clock face. The circle is, among other things, a symbol of unity. So the European flag was born, representing the ideal of unity among the peoples of Europe." [18]

However, on 28th October 2004, the Economist reported that Arsene Heitz, who designed the EU flag, got his inspiration from the woman described in the twelfth chapter of Revelation, who has twelve stars on her head.[19] Arsene Heitz is a Roman Catholic. The Roman Catholic religion interprets the woman to represent Mary. Therefore, the twelve stars on the EU flag seem to be the twelve-star halo of the Virgin

Mary seen in Roman Catholic art. In such paintings, you often see these twelve stars around Mary's head.

In the Bible, the antichrist and his kingdom are connected with Rome more than once. For example, the number of antichrist is 666:

> Here is wisdom. Let him who has understanding calculate the number of the beast, for it is the number of a man: His number is 666.
> (Revelation 13:18)

In the Hebrew Alphabet, each letter has a numerical value. Interestingly enough, in Hebrew, the numeric sums of both 'Roman [man]' and 'Roman Kingdom' are 666.

The Hebrew word for Roman [man] is 'Romiti':

R	=	200
O	=	6
M	=	40
I	=	10
T	=	400
I	=	10
		666

The Hebrew word for Roman Kingdom is 'Romiith':

R	=	200
O	=	6
M	=	40
I	=	10
I	=	10
TH	=	400
		666

Furthermore, the antichrist and his kingdom are portrayed in the book of Revelation as a beast with seven heads. In Revelation 17:9 the seven heads are said to be seven mountains, and a woman who represents a city is said to sit upon them.

> *Here is the mind which has wisdom: The seven heads are seven mountains on which the woman sits....And the woman whom you saw is that great city which reigns over the kings of the earth.*
> *(Revelation 17:9,18)*

I believe this immediately links the antichrist with Rome, as Rome was known as the 'seven hilled city' because of the seven mountains on which Rome was built. The names of the seven mountains were Capitolinus, Palatinus, Aventinus, Esquilinus, Coelius, Viminalis, and Quirinalis.

Furthermore, the woman is described as "that great city which reigns over the kings of the earth" (Revelation 17:18). The only city that reigned over the kings of the earth when the book of Revelation was written was Rome. The truth is that **the antichrist's kingdom will be a revised Roman Empire.**

In 800 AD, a man named Charlemagne attempted to revive the Roman Empire.[20] Charlemagne was the ruler of the Franks. Through military conquest, he became the undisputed ruler of Western Europe in 800 AD and was crowned by the pope. He restored much of the unity of the old Roman Empire and paved the way for the development of modern Europe. Interestingly, "the most important and renowned European award for distinguished service in the cause of Europe and European unification"[21] is called the International Charlemagne Prize. Why would this prize be named after Charlemagne? Could it be that Europe indeed sees itself as a revival of the old Roman Empire?

In September 2004, The Telegraph reported an EU exhibition. The headline was: "Art show sees Europe as 'new Roman Empire'". The pop-art collage was mounted in a tent outside the European Commission under the heading the "Roman Empire returns". The

Telegraph stated that "the display is not a formal expression of EU policy but it captures views that can be heard every day in the corridors and canteens of the Union's institutions".[22]

The EU Parliament building is in Strasbourg, France. The principal building is called the Louise Weiss building. It has been observed that its 60m high tower has a striking resemblance to Pieter Brueghel's 16th century *Tower of Babel* painting in Vienna's Kunsthistorisches Museum! The original Tower of Babel was never finished: in order to stop the people from building it, God caused confusion amongst them by causing them to speak in many languages for the first time, and they were scattered over all the earth (Genesis 11:1-9). Interestingly, the Louise Weiss building's tower has the appearance of being unfinished! Although the building is finished, the tower has been purposefully designed to appear unfinished.[23]

Josephus, the first century Jewish historian, informs us that a man named Nimrod led the movement to build the original Tower of Babel. Josephus informs us that after the flood, Nimrod challenged God to drown the world again, and that he would build a tower too high for the waters to reach, and that he would avenge on God for destroying their forefathers!

The place where they built the tower was called Babylon.[24] Interestingly, the woman in Revelation 17 who represents Rome is also called "Mystery, Babylon the Great".

> *And on her forehead a name was written: MYSTERY, BABYLON THE GREAT, THE MOTHER OF HARLOTS AND OF THE ABOMINATIONS OF THE EARTH.* (Revelation 17:5)

If the EU is the beginnings of a revised Roman Empire, how fitting it is that they already have a representation of Babylon's Tower of Babel as their Parliament's building!

As stated earlier, the antichrist's end time Roman Empire is depicted in Revelation 17 as a beast with a woman sitting on it. Interestingly, outside Europe's Council of Ministers office in Brussels there is also a sculpture of a woman riding a beast! Is Europe identifying itself as the antichrist's Roman Empire? The Greek two Euro coin also features a picture of a woman riding a beast (the Euro is the official currency of the Eurozone)!

Of course, the beast outside the Council of Ministers office and on the Greek two Euro coin does not have seven heads, and in Greek mythology, this imagery denotes the story of Europa being abducted by Zeus who came disguised as a bull. Nevertheless, the Bible also uses a similar image to denote Mystery Babylon and the end time Roman Empire.

So where is all of this heading? Denis MacShane (the Europe Minister) told the Financial Times that the German foreign minister was in favour of "giving all power to a new kind of European Kaiser [Ceasar]" who would "tell other European institutions what to do."[25] In the Roman Empire, the emperor was known as Caesar. Will the new Roman Empire (the EU) soon have its own Caesar? There are many who believe that one day, this Caesar will be the antichrist. Just in case that statement be seen as a little far fetched, consider the following statement made in 1957, which has been attributed to Paul-Henri Spaak, the former Belgian Prime Minister and President of the Consultative Assembly of the Council of Europe:

> *"We do not want another committee. We have too many already. What we want is a man of sufficient stature to hold the allegiance of the people, and to lift us out of the economic morass into which we are sinking. Send us such a man, and be he God, or the devil, we will receive him"* [26]

The original source for this quotation is uncertain. But what it does highlight is that desperate times call for desperate measures. When things get desperate enough, whether such desperation comes from the economy or other sources, the world will receive the leader who can solve their problems, no matter how wicked he is.

ECUMENISM

When the book of Revelation was written, the Roman Empire was experiencing a worldwide ecumenical movement i.e. a movement promoting worldwide unity among religions.[27] A Roman emperor had already built the Pantheon, which was a temple for all the gods, and so you could bring the religions together and unite the world religiously. However, the Christians would not join in with this, as Jesus cannot be placed alongside other gods.[28] Furthermore, the emperor Domitan (81-96 AD) demanded universal worship of himself. The penalty for not doing so was death. The Christians' refusal to comply with this resulted in further persecution. In fact, it was the advent of Domitan that inaugurated the fiercest attacks on Christians.[29] Many who refused to worship him were killed. It is against this backdrop that John receives the visions described in the book of Revelation. One such vision that is of particular interest in this chapter is found in Revelation 13:11-15:

> Then I saw another beast coming up out of the earth, and he had two horns like a lamb and spoke like a dragon. And he exercises all the authority of the first beast in his presence, and causes the earth and those who dwell in it to worship the first beast, whose deadly wound was healed. He performs great signs, so that he even makes fire come

down from heaven on the earth in the sight of men. And he deceives those who dwell on the earth by those signs which he was granted to do in the sight of the beast, telling those who dwell on the earth to make an image to the beast who was wounded by the sword and lived. He was granted power to give breath to the image of the beast, that the image of the beast should both speak and cause as many as would not worship the image of the beast to be killed. (Revelation 13:11-15)

Revelation 13 describes two beasts. The first is the antichrist, who will be the evil world ruler in the last days. The second beast is a false prophet, who will have the appearance of a righteous man ("two horns like a lamb"), but will in reality be a messenger of Satan ("and spoke like a dragon"). The false religious leader will cause the world to worship the antichrist, even as the Roman Empire worshipped the emperor. This false prophet will even be able to perform miraculous signs, by which he will deceive the world. Furthermore, like the Roman Empire of old, those who do not worship the antichrist will be killed.

The religious world in John's day was characterised by ecumenism and the worship of the emperor. It is no surprise that today, as the devil seeks to cause the Roman Empire to re-emerge, we see another worldwide ecumenical movement happening before our eyes. For example, on the 3rd January 2000, leaders from nine religious faiths in Britain stood together and made a public commitment to "work together for the common good... now and for generations to come".[30] The unprecedented event, hosted by the Prime Minister, brought together Christians, Jews, Muslims, Hindus, Buddhists, Sikhs, Baha'is, Jains, and Zoroastrians.

Another example of this trend is demonstrated by Prince Charles, who has already stated that he intends to be "Defender of Faith" instead of the "Defender of The Faith", which is the title of the British monarch. He does not regard Christianity as "the faith". However, we shouldn't get too attached to that title. The Pope originally gave the title "Defender of The Faith" to Henry VIII because he attacked the reformer Martin Luther, who was protesting against the Roman Catholic Church!

The former British Prime Minister, Tony Blair, also exhibits this ecumenical trend. On May 30th 2008, he launched the Tony Blair Faith Foundation, which will support inter-faith initiatives. On its committee are leaders from different religions.

Today, we are encouraged to believe that no one has a monopoly on the truth. It is said that no one religion has all the truth, though each has some. Consequently, all religions are seen as equally valid and necessary contributions to the health of our diverse world. I remember when as a child at school, we all went on a school trip to a Hindu temple. Whilst in the temple, we were encouraged to participate in one of the Hindu ceremonies. Fortunately, I refused to, but it demonstrates the subtle ways in which we were being encouraged to be embracive of each other's faith. Furthermore, religions are being encouraged to put aside their differences and work together for noble causes. We have already noted some examples of this. But another significant example occurred in Assisi on the 24th January 2002, where Pope John Paul II led 200 other religious leaders in a day of prayers for peace. Roman Catholic cardinals, Muslim clerics, Jewish rabbis, Buddhists, Sikhs, Bahais, Hindus, Jains, Zoroastrians and members of African traditional religions were among those gathered for prayer. However, the Bible does not teach us to unite with other religions, as Paul the apostle said:

> *Do not be unequally yoked together with unbelievers. For what fellowship has righteousness with lawlessness? And what communion has light with darkness?*
> *(2 Corinthians 6:14)*

It may seem somewhat harsh to refer to other religions as "lawlessness" and "darkness". But the Bible reveals that God is a jealous God, and He forbids the worship of any other god beside Himself (Exodus 20:2-6).

A danger when religions come together is compromise. In fact, on the day of prayer in Assisi, Franciscan monks **removed crosses** and other religious objects from rooms in a convent where some guests prayed![31]

In the midst of this ecumenical trend, it is essential that Christians do not compromise their faith. We must not bow to the pressure of accepting other religions' beliefs about the way to God. Only Jesus shed His blood for us, paying the ultimate price so that our sins could be forgiven, and thereby made a way for us to come to the Father. We are to maintain that Jesus is the only way to God the Father, as He Himself said:

> I am the way, the truth, and the life. No one comes to the Father except through Me.
> (John 14:6)

As the world's religions embrace one another, true Christianity which refuses to become one with other religions, will become less and less favourable within the world. In fact, in July 2000 it was reported that in France, missionaries and lay Christians who share their faith in Jesus could be imprisoned for up to two years under a planned French law that accuses religious proselytisers of "mental manipulation" of the public. French Justice Minister Elisabeth Guigou reportedly called the bill "a significant advance, giving a democratic state the legal tool [to] efficiently fight groups abusing its core values".[32]

We are living in a time where Christians, particularly in the West, must be ready to uphold the faith in the midst of persecution. It has been happening in other parts of the world for a long time, and in the West we have been somewhat sheltered from it. But there are signs emerging that the scene is changing, and we too need to be prepared for persecution. Here in the UK, in February 2009, it was reported that a five-year-old girl from Devon was left in tears after her teacher reprimanded her for talking about Jesus in class. Furthermore, governors are investigating her mother, who is a receptionist at the school, because she sent a personal email from home to friends at church asking them to pray about her daughter's situation![33] It was also reported in February 2009 that a Christian foster carer was struck off the fostering register because she allowed a Muslim child in her care to convert to Christianity.[34] In the same month, news emerged that a Christian nurse from Somerset had been suspended because she offered to pray for a patient.[35]

However, none of this should faze us. Rather, we should be encouraged. Jesus said:

> "Blessed are you when they revile and persecute you, and say all kinds of evil against you falsely for My sake. Rejoice and be exceedingly glad, for great is your reward in heaven, for so they persecuted the prophets who were before you."
> (Matthew 5:11 –12)

I believe that there is coming a time in Europe when Christians will be killed because of their faith. It is something that Christians need to consider seriously, and prepare themselves for accordingly. Ministers need to prepare their congregations.

That may seem far-fetched now, but we must remember that this is already happening in other countries. Furthermore, the Bible has already told us that the antichrist will persecute Christians, who will refuse to worship him:

> It was granted to him to make war with the saints and

to overcome them.
(Revelation 13:7)

Notice that the verse states that the antichrist will "overcome them". I understand this to simply mean that he will kill many Christians. Earlier in the book of Revelation, the martyrs were told that there were still more believers who were to be killed in the same way they had been (Revelation 6:11). As Christians, we must be willing to give up our lives for Christ. Are you?

END TIMES
ARE YOU PREPARED?

THE MARK OF THE BEAST

CHAPTER

Under the leadership of the antichrist, all people, regardless of social status, will be forced to receive a mark on their right hand or on their foreheads. Without this mark, people will not be able to buy or to sell. This "mark" is known as the mark of the beast, and is described in Revelation 13:16-18:

> *He causes all, both small and great, rich and poor, free and slave, to receive a mark on their right hand or on their foreheads, and that no one may buy or sell except one who has the mark or the name of the beast, or the number of his name.*
> *Here is wisdom. Let him who has understanding calculate the number of the beast, for it is the number of a man: His number is 666.*

The original Greek word translated "mark" literally means a scratch or etching i.e. a stamp (as in a badge of servitude).[36] It is the word used of the mark branded upon horses.[37] It thus appears to me that those who receive the mark are pledging their allegiance to the antichrist. Therefore, the Scriptures strongly warns us not to receive this mark:

> *Then a third angel followed them, saying with a loud voice, "If anyone worships the beast and his image, and receives his mark on his forehead or on his hand, he himself shall also drink of the wine of the wrath of*

God, which is poured out full strength into the cup of His indignation. He shall be tormented with fire and brimstone in the presence of the holy angels and in the presence of the Lamb. And the smoke of their torment ascends forever and ever; and they have no rest day or night, who worship the beast and his image, and whoever receives the mark of his name."
(Revelation 14:9-11)

The technology to manufacture the mark of the beast is already available. In a recent report on Dutch Television on Thursday, 7th October 2004 the reporter said:

"No more a wallet on a night out but paying with a implanted chip under the skin. That was yesterday night for the first time possible in the Baja Beach Club of Rotterdam. People who are willing to do so, can have a chip implanted in the upper arm. The chip is your entrance, your the admission ticket to the VIP-deck and your method of payment. The first customers got their chip implanted yesterday evening."[38]

Notice that the chip served as their method of payment. Without the mark of the beast, people will not be able to buy or sell. Whilst the Biblical text states that without the mark one cannot buy or sell, it doesn't specify the exact role the mark will play e.g. if it will act as an ID card granting the purchaser permission to use his/her cash, or if it will be more like a credit card. However, in light of the current direction of technology, it is likely that the mark will also be the method of payment.

VeriChip Corporation is one such organisation whose technology makes the mark of the beast a possibility. VeriChip Corporation was created in December 2001, after the events of 9-11. Firemen writing their badge ID on their chests in case they were found injured or unconscious revealed the difference an implantable microchip could make in emergency situations. VeriChip's microchip is about the size of a grain of rice and inserts just under the skin.

Unlike conventional forms of identification, the VeriChip cannot be stolen, misplaced, lost or counterfeited. The microchip contains a 16-digit electronic identifier, which can be used to access other personal information, such as medical records. VeriChip's solutions are currently in use in over 5,000 installations worldwide, crossing security, government, healthcare, and industrial markets. Presently, VeriChip provides solutions for patient identification, infant protection, and access control as well as other solutions.

Concerning VeriChip, Craig Offman of the Financial Times said:

"The VeriChip may be an extreme solution for extreme times, but the days it could be dismissed as futuristic fancy are clearly long past."[39]

VeriChip Corporation's website has several videos showing this technology in action. I have provided the direct Internet addresses of two such videos below. These addresses are correct at the time of writing:

http://www.verichipcorp.com/images/CNN_LouDobbs_021406.wmv
http://www.verichipcorp.com/files/CNN_AmerMorn_013106.wmv

They are both only a few minutes long, and make the above information come alive. There are also many other video clips available on their website.

Revelation 13:16-18 indicates that the mark of the beast will somehow be linked to the number 666.

Exactly how it will be linked is uncertain. However, it is possible that 666 may be encoded into the technology in some way. An example of this is found on the barcode that most products have. The lines on a barcode represent a number. The guard bars (at the beginning, middle, and end) on the barcode all resemble the barcode representation of the number 6. Therefore, it can be said that each barcode contains the appearance of the number 666. Of course, I am not saying that the barcode is the mark of the beast! It doesn't fully meet the description in Revelation 13:17-18. However, it is an example of how 666 can be encoded into a technology.

The implications of the mark of the beast are very serious – in order to buy and sell, we will need to have it. This includes buying food, which is a mandatory requirement for our survival! However, at the same time, we are warned that all who receive the mark will be punished with everlasting torment (Revelation 14:11). So, seeing as we are not to take the mark when it comes, how will we survive?

Some believe that before the mark of the beast comes, all who believe in Jesus will be 'raptured' and will meet the Lord in the air, and go to heaven whilst these things happen on the earth. Others believe that believers will be here when the mark of the beast comes. Whichever view one holds, the question of survival is still relevant. You see, the book of Revelation was originally written to seven churches based in Asia. It was written at a time when the Church was enduring great persecution. This persecution included financial persecution. For example, one of the churches the book of Revelation was originally written to was the church in Thyatira (Revelation 1:11). If you wanted to survive in Thyatira, you had to belong to a trade guild. Unless you belonged to a trade guild, you couldn't even open a shop. However, belonging to one of those trade guilds was incompatible with living a Christian lifestyle. Being part of a guild included pagan ceremonies, offering meat to idols, praying to a heathen god, and wild orgies. But if you did not join a trade guild, your business was finished.[40] Therefore, under such pressures, how are we to survive without compromising our faith? This question does not only belong to a future mark of the beast, it also belongs to the present time also. As stated in the first chapter of this book, over 200 million Christians in at least 60 countries are denied fundamental human rights solely because of their faith. We may not see this so much in the West, but I have received a first hand report from a pastor in India who shared that Christian children were being denied schooling because of their faith. So, how are we to financially survive without comprising our faith? Fortunately, Jesus showed us how, and we will answer this question in the next chapter.

END TIMES
ARE YOU PREPARED?

YOUR FINANCIAL SECURITY IN THE LAST DAYS

In the last chapter, we began to ask how we can financially survive in the last days. It ought to be noted at this point that God does not just want us to *survive*; He also wants us to *thrive* as indicated in the following passage:

> *Beloved, I wish above all things that thou mayest* **prosper** *and be in health, even as thy soul prospereth.*
> *(3 John 2, KJV emphasis added)*

Furthermore, in the context of financial giving, Paul wrote the following:

> *And God is able to make all grace abound toward you, that you, always having all sufficiency in all things, may have an abundance for every good work.*
> (2 Corinthians 9:8)

It is clear that God wants us to have "abundance". This means that we can have enough to meet our needs, and resources left over to the needs of others – "an abundance for every good work". This does not mean that our bank accounts always need to be full. When Jesus walked this earth, He didn't seem to carry a lot of cash. There is no indication that He had a big bank account anywhere. So, how did He survive? He simply used His Father's credit card! He always had His needs met and He was able to meet the needs of others, even feeding over 5,000 people! When He needed to pay His tax, He retrieved the money from a fish's mouth! We can see clearly that Jesus' financial security was not dependent upon any earthly system. God saw to it that Jesus was provided for, because Jesus always lived in the perfect will of God. In times of financial persecution and economic collapse, we can enjoy the same provision if we do the same. As I write, the world is experiencing unprecedented economic downturn. But thanks be to God, Jesus showed us the key to having all our needs met in Matthew 6:24-34. He said:

[24] *"No one can serve two masters; for either he will hate the one and love the other, or else he will be loyal to the one and despise the other. You cannot serve God and mammon.*
[25] *"Therefore I say to you, do not worry about your life, what you will eat or what you will drink; nor about your body, what you will put on. Is not life more than food and the body more than clothing?* [26] *Look at the birds of the air, for they neither sow nor reap nor gather into barns; yet your heavenly Father feeds them. Are you not of more value than they?* [27] *Which of you by worrying can add one cubit to his stature?*
[28] *"So why do you worry about clothing? Consider the lilies of the field, how they grow: they neither toil nor*

spin; ²⁹ *and yet I say to you that even Solomon in all his glory was not arrayed like one of these.* ³⁰ *Now if God so clothes the grass of the field, which today is, and tomorrow is thrown into the oven, will He not much more clothe you, O you of little faith?*
³¹ *"Therefore do not worry, saying, 'What shall we eat?' or 'What shall we drink?' or 'What shall we wear?'* ³² *For after all these things the Gentiles seek. For your heavenly Father knows that you need all these things.* ³³ *But seek first the kingdom of God and His righteousness, and all these things shall be added to you.* ³⁴ *Therefore do not worry about tomorrow, for tomorrow will worry about its own things. Sufficient for the day is its own trouble.*

The first thing we must realise is that we cannot serve both God and mammon (v24). The word 'mammon' is here used to describe money as a deity which people serve. Money must not be our god. We work, not because money is our god, but because God wants us to work to earn a living. Money, and the desire for it, must not be the driving force of our lives. In fact, God does not even need money in order to provide our needs. Therefore, we must not serve or love money, for "the love of money is a root of all kinds of evil" (1 Timothy 6:10) and, "those who desire to be rich fall into temptation and a snare, and into many foolish and harmful lusts which drown men in destruction and perdition" (1 Timothy 6:9).

The second thing we must realise is that we are not to worry (vs. 25-32). We are not to worry about what we shall eat and drink, what clothes we shall wear, or any of our material needs. Worry is an indicator of "little faith" (v30) and "without faith it is impossible to please Him" (Hebrews 11:6). If God provides for nature, then He will also provide for you, as you are of more value to God.

The third thing is given in verse 33, and is often the missing link in many people's lives:

> But seek first the kingdom of God and His righteousness, and all these things shall be added to you.
> (Matthew 6:33)

Jesus here tells us, that if we make the kingdom of God, and His righteousness, our first priority, "all these things" will be added to us. But, what is the kingdom of God? Too often, some think that Jesus is here referring to putting the Church first. As noble a thought as that is, that is not what Jesus is talking about here. This verse is found in Mathew chapter 6, and Jesus didn't start talking about the Church until ten chapters later in Matthew 16:18.

In a nutshell, the kingdom of God is the personal rule of God through Jesus Christ. Many of us in the West do not know what it is like to live in a kingdom, and therefore are unable to fully appreciate what Jesus is saying here. For example, here in Great Britain, we do not live in a kingdom. We live in what is called a *constitutional monarchy*.

In a constitutional monarchy, one person is the head of state (currently the Queen), and another person is the head of government (the Prime Minister). In other words, one person reigns, and another person rules! The Queen reigns, but the government rules. Many of us view God in that way. We freely acknowledge that God reigns. My challenge to you is, does God also rule in your life? Many people confess that God is King in their prayers and praises, but do not really live as though they are His subjects. They confess God reigns, but have not yielded do His rule – they refuse to be His subjects.

In a constitutional monarchy, the process of democracy elects the head of government. Ultimately, this means that the government derives its power from the people that elect it. Consequently, the government is seen as primarily serving the people. For example, in the run up to a general election, most people are asking "what will that government do for us?" You will not usually hear people asking, "what can we do for the government?" Unfortunately, there are people who approach God in this way also. They are only interested in what He can do for them, not in what they can do for Him. In other words, they are happy for the King to be their Saviour, but they are not willing to be His subjects.

A kingdom is very different than our constitutional monarchy. In a kingdom, the king reigns, and the king rules. The will of the king is law. He sits as king and his citizens are his subjects. The king does not derive his power from the people through a democratic election. He derives his power through inheritance. He is king because he is the son of a king.

To begin with, Jesus was very popular with the people. In fact, they soon wanted Him to be their king after the miracle of the loaves and fish.

Therefore when Jesus perceived that they were about to come and take Him by force to make Him king, He departed again to the mountain by Himself alone.
(John 6:15)

Jesus refused to allow them to make Him king. Why? It could be because Jesus knew that those people were not really His subjects. The people were looking for a king who would be their saviour, but the Saviour was looking for a people who would be His subjects. If we want Jesus to be our King, we must be willing to become His subjects. If you confess that God reigns, perhaps at this point you wish to ponder the question – does He also rule your life?

The kingdom of God is the personal rule of God, and that is what Jesus said we are to "seek first". This means we are to make it our number one priority. Our first priority must be to have God's personal rule established in our lives. This means that our desire must be to have our lives in perfect alignment with God's will. This is why Jesus taught us to pray, "Your kingdom come, your will be done..." (Matthew 6:10). When God's personal rule is established in our lives, everything we do will be in agreement with God's perfect will for us.

Seeking God's kingdom first does not mean that we should quit our jobs and simply "trust God" to provide our every need. If God has personally spoken to you to quit your job, so that you can dedicate yourself to the work of the ministry, then that is another matter.

However, the Bible does not commend laziness, and plainly states: "if anyone will not work, neither shall he eat" (2 Thessalonians 3:10).

Seeking God's kingdom first means that we surrender every part of our lives to His rule, and actively seek to bring our lives into alignment with His perfect will. This includes our careers, decisions, behaviour, education, finances, marriage, relationships... everything! Is every area of your life in perfect alignment with God's will? In order to seek God's kingdom first, your first priority must be to get those areas in alignment.

The personal rule of God is established in our lives by the Holy Spirit:

> ...the kingdom of God is not eating and drinking, but righteousness and peace and joy in the Holy Spirit. (Romans 14:17)

As we yield to the influence of the indwelling Holy Spirit, and seek His guidance, the kingdom of God is established in our lives. We must be sensitive to the Spirit's voice, to His promptings, to Him cautioning us against certain actions etc. We must cultivate sensitivity to Him by spending time in the Word, in prayer, and by walking in the Spirit, so that we can always recognise His voice.

When God's personal rule is our first priority, Jesus promises that the things we need will be provided. He doesn't specify how they will be provided, but promises that they will be - and we can be certain of His promise.

END TIMES
ARE YOU PREPARED?

ISRAEL

Israel has a very important place in end time prophecy and also in God's historical dealings with the world. There are many reasons for this, two of which are as follows:

1. They are the people from whom Jesus, the Saviour of the world, would be born.

2. They are the people to whom Jesus will return. When Jesus comes down to earth again, He will specifically touch down in Israel to defend the Jewish people.

The coming of the Lord Jesus spells the end for Satan. According to the pre-millennial interpretation of Biblical prophecy[41], the defeat of Satan will happen in three stages. The first stage was completed through the first coming of Jesus.

> *Inasmuch then as the children have partaken of flesh and blood, He Himself likewise shared in the same, that through death He might destroy him who had the power of death, that is, the devil*
> (Hebrews 2:14)

The Greek word translated "destroy" literally means to deprive of force, influence, and power.[42] This first stage means that through Jesus' death, people can now be free from the power of Satan.

The second stage of Satan's defeat will be completed at the Second Coming of Jesus Christ to the earth.

Then I saw an angel coming down from heaven, having the key to the bottomless pit and a great chain in his hand. He laid hold of the dragon, that serpent of old, who is the Devil and Satan, and bound him for a thousand years;
(Revelation 20:1-2)

Jesus will then rule the earth for 1,000 years, and Satan will be nowhere to be found. What a wonderful time that will be! After the thousand years, Satan will be loosed from his prison and will be cast into the lake of fire forever. This will be the third and final stage of Satan's defeat (Revelation 20:7-10).

Because the existence of the Jewish people is fundamental to both the first and second coming of Jesus, Satan has a special hatred for the Jewish people and has persecuted them many times throughout history. In the Old Testament, God warned the Jews that if they disobeyed His commandments, they would be punished. However, the devil wishes to take advantage of this situation. If Satan can succeed in wiping out the Jewish people, he thinks he can prevent the coming of the Messiah, and thus prevent his own defeat.

There are various historical examples of the Jews being persecuted. Here are just a few:

Pharoah - persecuted the Jews in Egypt, oppressing them and ordering their baby boys to be killed (see Exodus 1 – 14).

Haman - when the Jews were in ancient Persia, Haman tried to put an end to the Jewish people (Esther 3:5-6).

Antiochus Epiphanes - in 167 BC, he took over the Jewish temple and desecrated it. He established the worship of himself there instead.[43] He commanded that the Jews forsake their religious customs, forbidding them to sacrifice to God and keep holy days. All who did not obey were ordered to be killed. All who were found in possession of the Scriptures were also ordered to be killed. Therefore many Jews forsook their religion.[44]

Herod - ordered Jewish babies under 2 years old to be murdered (see Matthew 2:16).

The Roman Army - in AD 70, the Roman army

destroyed Jerusalem and the temple. Many Jews were killed. The Jewish people were scattered throughout the world.

Hitler – In more recent history, 6 million Jews were killed in the Holocaust.

Terrorist Attacks on Israel – There have been 80 terrorist attacks on Israel between 19th January 2006 and 22nd September 2008.[45]

Mahmoud Ahmadinejad - The current president of Iran declared that Israel should be "wiped off the map".[46] President Ahmadinejad has called the Holocaust a "myth" and has repeatedly called for Israel's elimination from time to time.[47]

However, Satan has not been able to succeed in wiping out the Jewish people. Jesus, who is the promised Jewish Messiah, predicted that the Jews would "fall by the edge of the sword, and be led away captive into all nations" (Luke 21:24). As mentioned above, this was fulfilled in AD 70: the Roman army destroyed Jerusalem and the temple, many Jews were killed and the Jewish people were scattered throughout the world. However, as evidence that Jesus the Messiah still intends on returning to the land and people of Israel, in recent history God has caused many of the Jews to return to their own land. The first Jewish settlement came to Palestine in 1879. By 1914 there were 40 Jewish settlements. By 1925, Jews were immigrating to Palestine at over 10,000 a year. On 14th May 1948, Israel was declared an independent nation.[48] Indeed, this reminds us of Ezekiel's prophecy, which was written between 593 – 573 BC when the Jews had been exiled to Babylon:

> *For I will take you from among the nations, gather you out of all countries, and bring you into your own land.* (Ezekiel 36:24)

However, Israel's troubles are by no means over. Paul predicts that when the antichrist comes to power, he will cause havoc in the Jewish temple:

> *He will oppose and will exalt himself over everything that is called God or is worshiped, so that he sets himself up in God's temple, proclaiming himself to be God.* (2 Thessalonians 2:4, NIV)

Paul predicts that the antichrist will exalt himself above all gods, sit in the temple and declare to be God. Paul here likens the antichrist to the ruler Antiochus Epiphanes (mentioned earlier) who in the 2nd century BC, took over the Jewish temple, desecrated it, and established there the worship of himself. The future antichrist will do likewise. Jesus predicted that this "abomination of desolation" would usher in a time of "great tribulation" and counselled that those in Judea should flee to the hills at this time:

"Therefore when you see the 'abomination of desolation,' spoken of by Daniel the prophet, standing in the holy place" (whoever reads, let him understand), "then let those who are in Judea flee to the mountains. Let him who is on the housetop not go down to take anything out of his house. And let him who is in the field not go back to get his clothes. But woe to those who are pregnant and to those who are nursing babies in those days! And pray that your flight may not be in winter or on the Sabbath. For then there will be great tribulation, such as has not been since the beginning of the world until this time, no, nor ever shall be.
(Matthew 24:15-21)

Daniel also predicted that the antichrist would cause the Temple sacrifices to stop (Daniel 9:27). Notice that all this presupposes that there will be a temple in Jerusalem in the last days. Presently there is not, and so in order for this prophecy to be fulfilled, the temple must be rebuilt, and the sacrifices must resume.

Today there exists a religious organisation located

in Jerusalem called the Temple Institute. On their website, they say, "Our short-term goal is to rekindle the flame of the Holy Temple in the hearts of mankind through education. Our long-term goal is to do all in our limited power to bring about the building of the Holy Temple in our time."[49]

According to some, this poses a potential problem. The site of the historic temple is known as Temple Mount, and presently, the Muslim Dome of the Rock mosque sits right there. However, the research of Israeli archaeologist Professor Joseph Patrich indicates that the rock over which the Dome of the Rock was built "is actually outside the confines of the Temple".[50]

Another obstacle has been that ashes of a red heifer are needed for the service of the Temple. The ashes of the red heifer were used with the water of cleansing (see Numbers 19:1-9). The problem is that red heifers have not existed for a long time. However, it has been reported that through genetic engineering, a herd of baby red cows are being raised under careful supervision.[51]

It has also been reported that animals have been purchased for ritual sacrifices at the site of the Temple.[52] However, the antichrist will cause these sacrifices to stop and will establish the worship of himself in the temple.

The Bible declares that God will execute judgments on the neighbours who despise Israel:

> 'Thus says the Lord GOD: "When I have gathered the house of Israel from the peoples among whom they are scattered, and am hallowed in them in the sight of the Gentiles, then they will dwell in their own land which I gave to My servant Jacob. And they will dwell safely there, build houses, and plant vineyards; yes, they will dwell securely, when I execute judgments on all **those around them who despise them**. Then they shall know that I am the LORD their God."'
> (Ezekiel 28:25-26)

Today, Israel is surrounded by nations that despise them. I recently saw a scarf from Jordan. The Arabic writing on the scarf said, "Jerusalem is ours, we're coming back". One does not have to look far to see the hatred many of the surrounding nations have towards the Jews. As we have already noted, between 19th January 2006 and 22nd September 2008, there have been 80 terrorist attacks on Israel. Furthermore, in response to the Israeli-Hamas conflict, many thousands of people across the world have gathered together in protest against Israel.

Many of the protesters held posters that declared their hatred for Israel, and their belief that Israel should be wiped off the map.

The Bible further reveals that just before Jesus returns, all nations will be gathered to battle against Jerusalem (Zechariah 14:2). Indeed, there have already been many claims that the United Nations is anti-Israel. For example, a 2005 report by the American Institute for Peace on UN reform states:

> *"Contrary to the equality of rights for all nations enshrined in the UN Charter, Israel continues to be denied rights enjoyed by all other member-states, and a level of systematic hostility against it is routinely expressed, organized, and funded within the United Nations system."*[53]

The Bible reveals that before the nations of the world jointly attack Jerusalem, they will first gather together at a place called Armageddon, which is north of Jerusalem. We read about Armageddon in Revelation 16:12-16:

> *Then the sixth angel poured out his bowl on the great river Euphrates, and its water was dried up, so that the way of the kings from the east might be prepared. And*

I saw three unclean spirits like frogs coming out of the mouth of the dragon, out of the mouth of the beast, and out of the mouth of the false prophet. For they are spirits of demons, performing signs, which go out to the kings of the earth and of the whole world, to gather them to the battle of that great day of God Almighty. "Behold, I am coming as a thief. Blessed is he who watches, and keeps his garments, lest he walk naked and they see his shame." And they gathered them together to the place called in Hebrew, Armageddon.

The river Euphrates will be dried up so that a route for those coming from the east to Armageddon can be prepared. Armageddon is otherwise known as the Valley of Jezreel. Napoleon (1769-1821) called this plain the world's greatest natural battlefield. He said there was sufficient room there for the armies of the world to manoeuvre.[54] How correct he was! This is precisely what will happen. The armies of the world will gather there before they proceed southward to attack Jerusalem. However, they will not be victorious, for Jesus Christ Himself will return to earth to defend Jerusalem. The outcome of this battle is described in Zechariah 14:2-13, which describes the Lord Jesus defending Jerusalem upon His future return to earth:

For I will gather all the nations to battle
against Jerusalem;
The city shall be taken,
The houses rifled,
And the women ravished.
Half of the city shall go into captivity,
But the remnant of the people shall not be cut off from the
city.
Then the LORD will go forth
And fight against those nations,
As He fights in the day of battle.
And **in that day His feet will stand on the Mount of Olives**,
Which faces Jerusalem on the east.
And the Mount of Olives shall be split in two,
From east to west,
Making a very large valley;
Half of the mountain shall move toward
the north
And half of it toward the south.
(Zech 14:2-4, emphasis added)

And the LORD shall be King over all the earth.
In that day it shall be—
"The LORD is one,"
And His name one.
(Zech 14:9)

> *And this shall be the plague with which the LORD will strike all the people who fought against Jerusalem:*
>
> *Their flesh shall dissolve while they stand on their feet,*
> *Their eyes shall dissolve in their sockets,*
> *And their tongues shall dissolve in their mouths.*
> *It shall come to pass in that day*
> *That a great panic from the LORD will be among them.*
> *Everyone will seize the hand of his neighbor,*
> *And raise his hand against his neighbor's hand;*
> *(Zech 14:12-13)*

As described in the above verses, this battle will be devastating for those who fight against Jerusalem. Perhaps you only view Jesus as being "meek and mild". However, the book of Revelation reveals that He is "clothed with a robe dipped in blood" and that the "armies of heaven" will follow Him when He returns to earth. He will "strike the nations" as He "judges and makes war" in righteousness (Revelation 19:11-15). The devastation of this war will be so great that there will be a great supper. However, instead of men gathering to eat the flesh of dead birds, it will be birds gathering to eat the flesh of dead men:[55]

> *Then I saw an angel standing in the sun; and he cried with a loud voice, saying to all the birds that fly in the midst of heaven, "Come and gather together for the*

supper of the great God, that you may eat the flesh of kings, the flesh of captains, the flesh of mighty men, the flesh of horses and of those who sit on them, and the flesh of all people, free and slave, both small and great." (Revelation 19:17-18)

In that battle, the antichrist and the false prophet will be captured and thrown into the lake of fire, which is also known as hell (Revelation 19:20). On that day, Jesus Christ will be established as King over all the earth and we will no longer need to pray, "Your kingdom come" (Matthew 6:10).

END TIMES
ARE YOU PREPARED?

A NEW HEAVEN AND A NEW EARTH

After Jesus defeats the armies that battled against Jerusalem, He will reign on the earth as King for 1,000 years. During this time, Satan will be bound, and the reign of Jesus will usher in a period of universal peace and prosperity, such as the earth has never before experienced. God's people will have already been resurrected, and the Bible specifically mentions that those who were killed because they refused to worship the antichrist, or take his mark, will reign with Christ. The prophet Isaiah described this period of time in the following way:

> He shall judge between the nations,
> And rebuke many people;
> They shall beat their **swords into plowshares**,
> And their **spears into pruning hooks**;
> Nation shall not lift up sword against nation,
> Neither shall they learn war anymore.
> (Isaiah 2:4, emphasis added)

As there will be no more war, weapons will be turned into agricultural instruments! Interestingly, in one of the United Nations Headquarters' gardens, there is a sculpture based on this verse. The sculpture was made by Yevgeny Vuchetich, and is of a man beating a sword into a ploughshare. However, this will never be fulfilled by the United Nations. This will only be fulfilled when Jesus returns and ushers in an era of peace.

The presence of Jesus Christ will also have a profound affect on wildlife:

> "The wolf also shall dwell with the lamb,
> The leopard shall lie down with the young goat,
> The calf and the young lion and the
> fatling together;
> And a little child shall lead them.
> The cow and the bear shall graze;
> Their young ones shall lie down together;
> And the lion shall eat straw like the ox.
> The nursing child shall play by the cobra's hole,
> And the weaned child shall put his hand in
> the viper's den.
> (Isaiah 11:6-8)

Animals will co-exist peacefully. Lions will be vegetarians, and children will be able to play safely near snakes! It will truly be a wonderful time.

After the 1,000 years, Satan will be released from his prison. He will deceive the nations, but fire from God will crush the satanic rebellion (Revelation 20:7-10). Satan will be thrown into the lake of fire, where the antichrist and the false prophet were also thrown when Jesus returned, and will be tormented there forever.

After this, the remaining dead will be resurrected. They will appear before God, and be judged according to their deeds. Anyone whose name is not found in the Lamb's Book of Life will be thrown into the lake of fire (Revelation 20:11-15).

After that, heaven and earth as we know it will pass away; and in their place will be a brand new heaven and earth. The focal point of this new creation will be a new city, called the New Jerusalem. The cowardly, the unbelievers, the corrupt, murderers, sexually immoral, those who practice witchcraft and sorcery, idol worshippers, and all liars, they will not be found here. Indeed, they will have been thrown into the lake of fire where they will be tormented forever, because they refused to repent. But those whose names have been written in the Book of Life will inhabit this new creation. God will wipe away every tear from their eyes. Here, there will be no more death, sorrow, crying, or pain. God Himself will dwell with humans. The New Jerusalem will not need a temple – God and His Son Jesus will be the temple. Nor will there be the need for the sun or moon – the glory God, and the Lord Jesus shall be its light, and there will be no night. Everything will be perfect. Its appearance will be beautiful, for the foundations of the jasper walls are adorned with all kinds of precious stones. The twelve gates are likened unto pearls, and the city is described as "pure gold, like clear glass". But most importantly, God Himself will be there, and His glory shall illuminate it (Revelation 21:1-27).

If you would like your name to be written in the Book of Life, so that you can spend eternity with God, then there are six steps you need to take:

1. Acknowledge that you are a sinner in rebellion against God. We have all sinned (i.e. disobeyed God) and have all walked contrary to God's righteousness:

for all have sinned and fall short of the glory of God
(Romans 3:23)

2. Understand that sin has a penalty:

For the wages of sin is death, but the gift of God is eternal life in Christ Jesus our Lord
(Romans 6:23)

3. Believe that Jesus Christ died on the cross so that your sins could be forgiven. Because we have all sinned, we all deserved to have been on the cross.

However, Jesus voluntarily took our place, and paid sin's penalty for us all:

> But God demonstrates His own love toward us, in that while we were still sinners, Christ died for us
> (Romans 5:8)

4. Confess your sins to God:

> If we confess our sins, He is faithful and just to forgive us our sins and to cleanse us from all unrighteousness.
> (1 John 1:9)

5. Repent of your sins. To repent means to have a complete change of attitude towards sin. Decide that with God's help you will no longer live a sinful lifestyle, and that you will not live a life that is independent of God.

> ...unless you repent you will all likewise perish
> (Luke 13:3)

6. Confess Jesus Christ as your Saviour and Lord. Give Him control of your life:

> ...if you confess with your mouth, "Jesus is Lord," and believe in your heart that God raised him from the dead, you will be saved. For it is with your heart that you

believe and are justified, and it is with your mouth that you confess and are saved. (Romans 10:9-10, NIV).

To help you activate those six steps, please pray the following prayer out loud, praying from the depths of your heart:

Dear God,

You are the Creator of all things. I acknowledge that I am a sinner in rebellion against You, and that I deserve Your punishment. Thank you that Jesus Christ died on the Cross for my sins so that I could be forgiven. Today, I ask you to forgive my sins. I repent of my sins today, and make a decision to live for You, and to no longer live a sinful lifestyle. I confess that Jesus Christ is Lord and give Him full control of my life. I receive Jesus as my personal Saviour today. Thank you for saving me.

In Jesus' name,
Amen.

Congratulations! Now that you have prayed that prayer from your heart, your sins have been forgiven, your name has been written in the Book of Life, and you have begun an exciting journey with the Lord. Be sure to find a local church that you can attend each week, where the Bible is taught, you can worship God, and enjoy fellowship with other believers. Be sure to read the Bible each day, and to pray to God, asking for His help in all you do.

Please also feel free to visit **www.stuartpattico.com** where you can find useful articles to help you on your journey.

God bless you.

END TIMES
ARE YOU PREPARED?

WILL YOU BE READY?

In this closing chapter, I would like to challenge you with a simple question: will you be ready when Jesus comes? The apostle Paul beautifully described what will happen when Jesus comes to meet the Church in the air:

> For the Lord Himself will descend from heaven with a shout, with the voice of an archangel, and with the trumpet of God. And the dead in Christ will rise first. Then we who are alive and remain shall be caught up together with them in the clouds to meet the Lord in the air. And thus we shall always be with the Lord.
> (1 Thessalonians 4:16-17)

However, Jesus warned us that we must be ready for this event:

> Therefore you also be ready, for the Son of Man is coming at an hour you do not expect.
> (Luke 12:40)

Jesus will come at an hour we are not expecting Him. Jesus then went on to illustrate what it means to be ready, and the consequences of not being ready:

> ⁴² And the Lord said, "Who then is that faithful and wise steward, whom his master will make ruler over his household, to give them their portion of food in

due season? ⁴³ Blessed is that servant whom his master will find so doing when he comes. ⁴⁴ Truly, I say to you that he will make him ruler over all that he has. ⁴⁵ But if that servant says in his heart, 'My master is delaying his coming,' and begins to beat the male and female servants, and to eat and drink and be drunk, ⁴⁶ the master of that servant will come on a day when he is not looking for him, and at an hour when he is not aware, and will cut him in two and appoint him his portion with the unbelievers. ⁴⁷ And that servant who knew his master's will, and did not prepare himself or do according to his will, shall be beaten with many stripes.
(Luke 12:42-47)

Those who have been living right will receive a great reward when Jesus returns. However, those who have not will be dealt with accordingly. In Jesus' illustration, the good servant was ready for his master's return because he had an important habitual characteristic: he did the will of his master.

Blessed is that servant whom his master will find so doing when he comes
(v43)

You too will be ready, if you habitually do the same. You must do what the Lord has instructed you to do. If this is your lifestyle, then you will be ready when

He comes.

But what does it mean to do our master's will? In terms of ministry, it means that we are doing what God has called and gifted us to do. Perhaps God has called you to be an evangelist. Are you fulfilling that calling? Perhaps God has called you to work with the poor. Are you fulfilling that calling? Whatever God has gifted and called you to do, it is important that you are obedient to that calling:

> *For as we have many members in one body, but all the members do not have the same function, so we, being many, are one body in Christ, and individually members of one another. Having then gifts differing according to the grace that is given to us, let us use them*
> *(Romans 12:4-6)*

However, doing the will of God goes beyond our ministry. Our conduct and behaviour must also be in agreement with God's will. We must not only ask ourselves, "Am I doing what God has called me to do?" We must also ask, "Am I behaving in the way God wants me to behave?" Let us ever be mindful of Jesus' stern words in Matthew 7:

> *"Not everyone who says to Me, 'Lord, Lord,' shall enter the kingdom of heaven, but he who does the will of My*

Father in heaven. Many will say to Me in that day, 'Lord, Lord, have we not prophesied in Your name, cast out demons in Your name, and done many wonders in Your name?' And then I will declare to them, 'I never knew you; depart from Me, you who practice lawlessness! (Matthew 7:21-23)*

You can have a powerful ministry, but if you "practice lawlessness" you are not doing "the will of My Father in heaven". But what does it mean to practice lawlessness?

The term "lawlessness" includes any violation of God's laws. Whilst we are no longer under the Law of Moses, there are still certain standards by which God expects His people to live, and God's standard is no lower today than it was in the Old Testament. For example, the Bible teaches that as Christians we should always tell the truth. We are not to lie (Colossians 3:9). We are not to steal (Ephesians 4:28). We are not to murder (Romans 13:9). We are to honour authority (Romans 13:1-7). We are not to engage in sexual relationships outside of marriage (1 Corinthians 10:8). We are not to gossip (Ephesians 4:29). We are not to seek revenge, but are to bless those who curse us, and do good to those who do bad to us (Matthew 5:43-48, Romans 12:19-21). Jesus said,

> *Therefore, whatever you want men to do to you, do also to them, for this is the Law and the Prophets.*
> (Matthew 7:12)

As far as our relationships with others are concerned, the Old Testament Law and Prophets can be summarised by saying this: treat others in the way you wish to be treated. Therefore, when we mistreat others, we are practicing lawlessness. And if we practice lawlessness, we will not enter the kingdom of heaven.

Our conduct is just as important as our ministries. We should not be one thing in ministry, and another in conduct. Therefore, Jesus was careful to warn His disciples of a potential danger that threatens us all – hypocrisy.

> *...Jesus began to speak first to his disciples, saying: "Be on your guard against the yeast of the Pharisees, which is hypocrisy.*
> (Luke 12:1, NIV)

Hypocrisy is simply claiming to have standards or beliefs that are contrary to your real character and actual behaviour.[56] However, in the next two verses, Jesus made it clear that one day, everything we have done in private will be made public, and all will see who we really are:

> There is nothing concealed that will not be disclosed, or hidden that will not be made known. What you have said in the dark will be heard in the daylight, and what you have whispered in the ear in the inner rooms will be proclaimed from the roofs.
> (Luke 12:2-3, NIV)

It is interesting that Jesus referred to hypocrisy as the yeast of the Pharisees. They were religious leaders, yet many of them were hypocrites. Perhaps you are a church member and have been faithful over the years in tithing and fasting. However, this does not mean that you are doing the will of God, for the Pharisees were faithful in these same practices! Consider the following parable taught by Jesus:

> Also He spoke this parable to some who trusted in themselves that they were righteous, and despised others: "Two men went up to the temple to pray, one a Pharisee and the other a tax collector. The Pharisee stood and prayed thus with himself, 'God, I thank You that I am not like other men—extortioners, unjust, adulterers, or even as this tax collector. **I fast twice a week; I give tithes of all that I possess.**' And the tax collector, standing afar off, would not so much as raise his eyes to heaven, but

beat his breast, saying, 'God, be merciful to me a sinner!' I tell you, this man went down to his house justified rather than the other; for everyone who exalts himself will be humbled, and he who humbles himself will be exalted."
(Luke 18:9-14, emphasis added)

This Pharisee faithfully tithed and fasted. But, because of his pride he is described as praying "with himself"! Therefore, in order to be ready for Christ's coming, we need to humble ourselves before God continually, crying out for His mercy as the tax collector did. The good news in this parable is that the tax collector went away justified. It is wonderful to know that if we do get things wrong; we can confess our sins to God with a repentant attitude and receive His forgiveness. However, if we walk in pride, we are deceived, and will not be ready for our Saviour's coming.

I would like to close this book by asking you to do something. Humble yourself before God and ask yourself this question, "If the Lord were to come now, would I be ready?" Allow the Holy Spirit to show you things in your life that are not pleasing to Him. Ask for God's forgiveness where needed, and receive God's grace, enabling you to do His will.

CONTACT INFORMATION AND ENDNOTES

CONTACT INFORMATION AND ENDNOTES

Stuart Pattico is available for speaking engagements, and his wife, Andrea, is available to minister at worship events. To contact either of them, or if you would like to be added to their mailing list, please use the contact form on their website:

www.stuartpattico.com

CHAPTER 1: SIGNS OF THE TIMES

[1] David Pawson, *When Jesus Returns* (London: Hodder & Stoughton Ltd, 2003) page 2.

[2] World Food Program, http://wfp.org/aboutwfp/introduction/hunger_what.asp?section=1&sub_section=1 (accessed 8 April 2009).

[3] AVERT (an international AIDS charity), http://www.avert.org/worldstats.htm (accessed 8 April 2009).

[4] Derek Prince, *Orphans, Widows, the Poor and Oppressed* (Derek Prince Ministries – UK, 2006), page 37.

[5] U.S. Geological Survey, http://neic.usgs.gov/neis/eqlists/graphs.html (accessed 4 April 2009).

[6] West Coast and Alaska Tsunami Warning Center, http://wcatwc.arh.noaa.gov/tsustats.pdf (accessed 4 April 2009).

[7] Every Child Matters: Change for Children, http://www.everychildmatters.gov.uk/_files/47053059F3064C19FDD119F09BFDAE00.doc (accessed 4 April 2009) based on provisional 2007 data.

[8] Revival Times, September 2002, http://www.revivaltimes.org/index.php?aid=493 (accessed 5 April 2009).

[9]Release International, http://www.releaseinternational.org/pages/find-out-more/christian-persecution-faqs.php (accessed 5 April 2009).

CHAPTER 2: GLOBALISATION

[10] Taipei Times, http://www.taipeitimes.com/News/editorials/archives/2006/02/21/2003294021 (accessed 6 April 2009).

[11] Peter Gates, *Issues in Mathematics Teaching* (Routledge, 2002) page 205.

[12] Telegraph, http://www.telegraph.co.uk/finance/financetopics/financialcrisis/3414516/Gordon-Brown-world-leaders-should-create-truly-global-society.html (accessed 9 April 2009).

[13] BBC News, http://news.bbc.co.uk/1/hi/uk_politics/7850649.stm (accessed 13 March 2009).

[14] Time Magazine, October 21st 1974, http://www.time.com/time/magazine/article/0,9171,945020,00.html (accessed 8 April 2009). For more information, please refer to the original book *Mankind at the Turning Point: The Second Report to the Club of Rome* by Mihajlo D Mesarovic and Eduard Pestel.

[15] Telegraph, http://www.telegraph.co.uk/finance/financetopics/g20-summit/5097195/G20-summit-Gordon-Brown-announces-new-world-order.html (accessed 4 April 2009).

CHAPTER 3: EUROPE

[16] European NAvigator, *Political Resolution of the Hague Congress* (7 – 10 May 1948), http://www.ena.lu/ (accessed 6 April 2009). The statement is found in the World Unity paragraph of this political resolution.

[17] EU Website, STRATEGIC OBJECTIVES 2000-2005 "Shaping the New Europe" © European Communities, 1995-2009, http://ec.europa.eu/comm/off/work/2000-2005/com154_en.pdf (accessed 6 April 2009).

[18] EU Website, http://europa.eu/abc/symbols/emblem/index_en.htm (accessed 22 December 2008)

[19] Economist, http://www.economist.com/world/europe/displaystory.cfm?story_id=E1_PPPNDVG (accessed 17 April 2009).

[20] Charlemagne founded the Holy Roman Empire, which was an attempt to revive the Western Roman Empire. Encarta, http://uk.encarta.msn.com/encyclopedia_761558731/holy_roman_empire.html (accessed 17 April 2009).

[21] Charlemagne Prize website, http://www.karlspreis.de/index.php?id=172 (accessed 20 December 2008).

[22] Telegraph, http://www.telegraph.co.uk/news/worldnews/europe/1471722/Art-show-sees-Europe-as-new-Roman-Empire.html (accessed 15 April 2009).

[23] Pictures of Brueghel's painting and the Louise Weiss building can be seen on various Internet sites.

[24] Flavius Josephus, *The Antiquities of the Jews*, Book 1, Chapter 4.

[25] Telegraph, http://www.telegraph.co.uk/news/worldnews/europe/france/1417796/British-outburst-on-'EU-Kaiser'-upsets-Germans.html (accessed 22 December 2008).

[26] David Jeremiah, *What in the World Is Going On?: 10 Prophetic Clues You Cannot Afford to Ignore* (Thomas Nelson Inc, 2008) page 65.

CHAPTER 4: ECUMENISM

[27] The Free Dictionary, The American Heritage® Dictionary, Fourth Edition copyright ©2000 by Houghton Mifflin Company. Updated in 2003. Published by Houghton Mifflin Company. All rights reserved. http://www.thefreedictionary.com/ecumenism (accessed 5 April 2009). Please note that in this book, 'ecumenism' is not used to refer to the uniting of Bible-believing Christians.

[28] David Pawson, *Come With Me Through Revelation* (Terra Nova Publications, 2008) page 24.

[29] David Pawson, *Unlocking the Bible* (London: HarperCollinsPublishers, 2003) page 1267.

[30] The Inter Faith Network for the UK, http://www.interfaith.org.uk/rcommit.htm (accessed 16 April 2009).

[31] BBC News, http://news.bbc.co.uk/1/hi/world/europe/1779135.stm (accessed 8 January 2009).

[32] BBC News, http://news.bbc.co.uk/1/hi/world/europe/802070.stm (accessed 4 April 2009).

[33] The Christian Institute, http://www.christian.org.uk/news/20090212/teacher-scolds-girl-5-for-talking-about-jesus/ (accessed 5 March 2009).

[34] The Christian Institute, http://www.christian.org.uk/news/20090208/christian-carer-struck-off-after-muslim-girl-converts/ (accessed 5 March 2009).

[35] The Christian Institute, http://www.christian.org.uk/news/20090202/diversity-rules-see-nurse-suspended-for-prayer-offer/ (accessed 5 March 2009).

CHAPTER 5: THE MARK OF THE BEAST

[36] Strong's Bible Dictionary, courtesy of e-Sword® software

[37] Thayer's Greek Definitions, courtesy of e-Sword® software

[38] Infowars, http://www.infowars.com/print/bb/baja_netherlands.htm (accessed 8 January 2009).

[39] VeriChip's website, http://www.verichipcorp.com/content/company/our_technology (accessed 4 April 2009).

[40] David Pawson, *Come With Me Through Revelation* (Terra Nova Publications, 2008) pages 97 – 98.

CHAPTER 7: ISRAEL

[41] The pre-millennial interpretation holds that Jesus will come before the thousand-year period described in Revelation 20. The post-millennial interpretation believes that Jesus will come afterwards. This amillennial interpretation views the thousand-year period symbolically, and as identical with the current church age.

[42] Thayer's Greek Definitions, courtesy of e-Sword® software.

[43] N. T. Wright, *The New Testament and the People Of God* (London: Society for Promoting Christian Knowledge, 2004) page 158.

[44] See the Apocryphal book 1 Maccabees.

[45] Johnston's Archive, http://www.johnstonsarchive.net/terrorism/terrisrael-10.html (accessed 2 December 2008).

[46] CNN, http://www.cnn.com/2005/WORLD/meast/10/26/ahmadinejad/ (accessed 5 October2008).

[47] MSN, http://news.uk.msn.com/Article.aspx?cp-documentid=8528096 (accessed 24 September 2008).

[48]Ed Rayner and Ron Stapley, *World History* (Essex: Addison Wesley Longman Ltd, 1997) pages 265 – 267.

[49]The Temple Institute, http://www.templeinstitute.org/about.htm (accessed 9 October 2008).

[50]The Jerusalem Post, http://www.jpost.com/servlet/Satellite?cid=1170359807477&pagename=JPost%2FJPArticle%2FShowFull (accessed 13 September 2008).

[51]David Silver, *A Slow Train Coming* (Rhema Media Centre, 2002) page 123.

[52]Worthy News, http://worthynews.com/news/haaretz-com-hasen-spages-831646-html/ (accessed 9 October 2008).

[53]United States Institute of Peace, *American Interest and UN reform*. REPORT OF THE TASK FORCE ON THE UNITED NATIONS, http://www.usip.org/un/report/usip_un_report.pdf (accessed 6 April 2009).

[54]J. Dwight Pentecost, *Prophecy For Today* (Michigan: Zondervan Publishing House, 1976) page 140.

[55]David Pawson, *Come With Me Through Revelation* (Terra Nova Publications, 2008) page 293.

CHAPTER 9: WILL YOU BE READY?

[56] The Free Dictionary, Collins Essential English Dictionary 2nd Edition 2006 © Harper Collins Publishers 2004, 2006, http://www.thefreedictionary.com/Hypocrisy (accessed 5 April 2009).